Relationship Secrets
That Really Work

By: Nora and Jim Zarvos
[Transformational Trainers
Married with Children]

Preface

Many people approach relationships with an idyllic picture of how things are going to be. When that picture does not meet up with reality, they can suddenly find themselves struggling in an ocean of confusion, boredom, frustration, sadness, and even anger. The result is communication gets stifled, walls get built, and two people within an arm's reach end up being miles apart.

But, it does not have to be this way.

We have written this book to help you create the relationship you really want to have with your partner or spouse. Imagine a relationship filled with renewed passion, trust and intimacy. It *can* be yours—you just need to be equipped with the right set of tools and strategies to support your vision.

Have you have ever seen a couple who were still crazy about each other after being together for years? Do you wonder how they got there? What is their secret?

The secret is *successful* couples approach relationships differently than unsuccessful couples. Successful couples utilize a cohesive set of practices and strategies that promote positive experiences, encourage communication, and embrace personal differences. It matters not whether their practices and strategies are conscious or unconscious. In every healthy relationship you will find these same practices and principles in place.

In this book you will learn what these principles are—and how to apply them. While this book primarily deals with a primary relationship, these principles apply to any relationship you have with others—your relatives, friends, kids, and co-workers.

The principles and practices that you are about to learn are time-tested strategies that we personally use within our marriage and have taught to tens of thousands of our workshop attendees. It has been a true pleasure to watch as our workshop participants transform themselves and their personal relationships as a result.

Our intent is that this book will provide answers to some of your most burning questions, and will empower you to transform your primary and secondary relationships into bright flourishing experiences.

You have chosen to read this book for a reason. Thank you, on behalf of those you love, for taking the time to create an experience that will

make any relationship truly worth committing
to.

Jump in, and know your journey to mastering a
joyful, meaningful, and connected relationships
is about to begin!

Table of Contents

Introduction

Let's start off with a sobering fact: statistically speaking most relationships these days end in failure. Even successful couples will tell you that maintaining a healthy relationship takes a lot of hard work, patience, and persistence.

So the question is, why bother? Why put yourself out there? Is an intimate relationship really worth all the time, effort and risk involved?

Instinctively, you already know the answer to this question. After all, *you* made the choice to read to this book.

We all have a primal, innate desire for life. But, if we are truly going to *live* our life, then we simply cannot ignore the central role that our relationship with others plays in it. **The**

quality of our life is directly related to the quality of our day-to-day experiences, and some of the most important experiences we will ever have are those that we share with others— especially our partner or spouse.

Relationships in Breakdown

Today, the sacred pillar of marriage and long-term intimate relationships is crumbling. Within several major Western countries including the U.S., almost 50 percent of first marriages end in divorce. The odds of success are even worse for people who have been married more than once: nearly three quarters of second and third marriages within the U.S. end in divorce.

The end of a marriage or long-term relationship causes enormous upheaval— mentally, spiritually and physically. The courts are full of acrimonious couples in conflict over their split-up that leaves a wake of irreversible devastation.

A Rise in Expectations

There are a couple primary reasons why so many people fail in their most intimate relationships. Number one on the list is the **expectations** we and society place on our relationships are higher than ever. Conversely, the higher our expectations, the greater the disappointment we feel when they are unmet.

Once upon a time, people got married to increase the odds of survival in a *physically* harsh world. If one marriage partner didn't survive (through disease, accident, tribal warfare, etc.) at least there would be someone left to care for the children who were necessary to ensure the survival of the family, species, and community.

Of course, few of us today go into an intimate relationship because we are worried about where our next meal is going to come from, or whether we are going to be attacked by a wild animal. Beyond the need for physical survival, procreation, or even our social desire for connection, support, and affection; we are now looking for a partner to make us feel happy, fulfilled, and ultimately feel good about ourselves.

Whether we realize it or not, most of us are going through life attempting to increase the odds of survival in an *emotionally* harsh world. This is a paradigm that eats up our self-esteem, and usually leaves us feeling empty, deflated, and disconnected from ourselves—as well as those around us.

By taking our arduous expectations and placing

them squarely on the shoulders of our most intimate social connections, there is little wonder why so many relationships fail! When our needs for self-acceptance, fulfillment, and happiness are not met, it is easy to become disenchanted with our partner and not realize what the real problem is.

We end up recreating an ongoing cycle of disconnection and dissatisfaction—a reality that is miles apart from what Hollywood tells us our relationships should look and feel like. In comparison, life with our partner will appear to be mundane and stale.

The end result is that most people suffer through relationships where they experience far less happiness and fulfillment than they actually could achieve had they instead operated from time-tested relationship practices.

Growing Complexity of Roles

In my parents' generation, dad went to work to earn the money, while mom stayed at home to take care of the children and run the house. Everyone knew their role and there was security and comfort for all concerned, if they fulfilled those roles effectively. Today, however, our roles and relationships are far more diverse and complicated than they have ever been.

The same loss of clear roles has also crept into the business world. We coach many of today's business leaders on creating high-performance teams. The lack of well-defined roles and responsibilities is typically one of the major dysfunctions. Business teams are always composed of individuals possessing different personalities, backgrounds, and talents.

In addition, teams are often cross-functional

and are comprised of people from various departments, physical locations, and cultures. In order for the business team to be successful, all the individuals must work together to create specific results that ultimately bring value to the business. As with any couple, when a team member's roles and responsibilities are not clearly defined, it can quickly lead to a breakdown in communication and an assortment of misaligned behaviors that can keep the whole team from achieving its goals.

In today's world, simple solutions to our complex problems have taken the back seat to quick fixes that treat the symptoms rather than the cause. The result is that many people tend to cope with the pain they are feeling by breaking off the relationship, having an affair, burying themselves in their work, or by denying the problems that are smacking them in the face.

From Coping to Practicing

The crux of the issue is that many of us were never taught the tools and skills we need to make our relationships work. Instead, we are caught in the unfulfilling cycle of passive acceptance and coping.

Thus, the real answer to today's relationship challenge is to learn the factors that *cause* relationships to thrive and then consistently work to put that knowledge into practice. In other words, both individuals have to be committed to creating a space that promotes healthy communication, allows for constructive disagreement, and is a wellspring of support, encouragement and mutual giving.

How is Your Relationship Today?

Take a few minutes and think about your current relationship. First, get in touch with how things were at the beginning. Do you remember the first time you and your partner met? Remember and reconnect to the excitement and passion that came with meeting this person—falling in love, discovering each other, and sharing new experiences. Sit with your feelings for a couple of minutes.

How does this compare to the way things are today? Is there still an element of newness and excitement in your relationship? Are you still overflowing with feelings of love and connection towards this person? Though we hope that you are responding with a resounding "yes," we would not be surprised if this is not the case. We cannot tell you how many couples we have met who are in a relationship where the passion is gone or worse—where there is jealousy, bitterness, and constant arguing.

If you and your partner fit the latter description then take out a piece of paper and a pencil. Over the next 10 minutes write down every excuse you can think of that justifies your current situation and explain why your relationship is lacking. For example, your list might look something like this:

- *"We've been together for a while and I know everything about him/her. There's really nothing new to keep our relationship interesting and exciting anymore."*

- *"Real life got in the way—children, finances, career, friends and family.*

There's so much competing for my attention that I don't have the time or the energy to focus on my relationship."

- *"We're both older now and our hormones have leveled off."*

- *"It's normal for a relationship to get boring at some stage."*

- *Actually, our sex life is pretty good. It's better than most."*

- *"I'd rather be with someone than be alone."*

- *"We are just going through a   phase right now – it will get better someday."*

When you are done building your list, look it over and be with it for a while.

Now there is an important truth for you to consider:

Neither of us has *ever* seen change, transformation, or success occur while people continue to breathe life into their excuses and justifications. The very purpose of these justifications is to maintain the current situation.

Take a moment and reflect on this statement before moving on

.

Building the Foundation

Perhaps your list has gotten the wheels turning in your head, and you have already begun planning how you are going to successfully "fix" or "transform" the situation. Not so fast!

First, consider the following analogy:

Imagine you are sitting in your living room and you notice you have a large crack in one of the walls. How would you go about repairing that crack?

One solution would be to go to the hardware store and ask for advice on how to fix the wall. You might be told to buy some plaster, fill in the crack, and then paint or wallpaper over it. Problem solved. Or would it be? Two weeks later, you notice that another crack has appeared on the same wall. Again, you could fill in that crack and any others that show up. But, if your wall is being overrun by cracks, then chances are you have a more fundamental problem.

A better approach would be to ask, "*What is **causing** these cracks to appear in the first place?*" The answer to that question would call for some deeper investigation. You would now want to examine the entire structure of the house, the foundation, and the land the house is sitting on. If you discover that two piers are sinking and that both need to be replaced or shored up, it can at first be difficult to accept such a large and expensive repair. But, the fact is that once the foundation of your house is restored, no further cracks will appear. Your house will now do what it is supposed to do, provide you with the shelter, security, and the peace of mind you seek.

Relationships work the same way. If you only focus on soothing the unhappiness and distress without trying to identify the root cause, then you will basically spend your time "papering over the cracks." You will be wasting precious time and energy trying to "fix" the problem all the while wondering why the same issues keep resurfacing over and over again.

Pillars for Success

The biggest takeaway from all of this is that in order for any relationship to be successful, a solid foundation must be built. Once that foundation is in place, you can then begin to nurture and grow your relationship in a solid, stable way. If you get it right, then even when a storm or circumstances that feel like an earthquake come along, you will be able to weather the storm, without worrying that every struggle you face will tear the whole structure of your relationship apart.

So let's jump into it. In order to build a proper foundation for your relationship there are five fundamental pillars that must be in place:

The First Pillar: Personal Responsibility

The foundation of a healthy relationship starts with *you*. The core principle of having a relationship that is loving and joyful is taking 100% responsibility for the entire *relationship*. While we agree that it takes "two to tango," we say that it only takes one to be the catalyst.

Your relationship will never thrive, nor will solutions ever arise when you are blaming the other. Blame has never been the source of a solution. Taking ownership of what's occurring in the relationship with an intent to cause a positive outcome is a secret hidden from most individuals.

Take for an example those teachers who are teaching in highly dysfunctional schools who manage to turn out highly educated students year in and year out. It always starts with their willingness to take responsibility for their student's learning and education. It is the same in business. Business leaders know they cannot be sort of responsible for the results caused by the people they lead and manage. Successful leaders understand personal responsibility is a non-negotiable success principle and are empowered by the idea that they can manifest outcomes consistent with their visions.

We are not in disagreement with the idea that in any relationship there are two people individually making choices that affect the other. We are highlighting a relationship secret which is embedded in the habits of all successful couples. Without exception at least one, if not both, take ownership of the relationship in its entirety and are willing to do whatever it takes to ensure the outcomes are consistent with their vision of relationship success.

The Second Pillar: Know Yourself

It is to your benefit to realize that your relationship with your partner is a perfect reflection of the relationship you have with yourself. There is no way around it. How we see ourselves is how we see our world; how we see others is what we really see in ourselves (yep, the good, the bad, and... the ugly). Yet ironically, self-knowledge is the most overlooked and under emphasized aspect of intimate relationships. So take the advice of the ancient statement inscribed in the Temple of Apollo and "Know Thy Self."

What do **YOU** want in life? What core values drive you? What holds you back? What do you still need to learn? It's important to reflect on these formative questions.

The Third Pillar: Know Your Partner

One of the most exciting aspects of an intimate relationship is not just the self-discovery that will happen along the way, but also the simultaneous discovery and appreciation of your partner that also occurs.

As is always the case, you can see things in your partner that he or she will not be able to see. As you go about building your relationship, get to know what your partner desires in life. What drives and inspires your partner? What holds this person back? What is this person afraid of? What does your partner need or want from you?

One of the biggest keys to a successful relationship is to become conscious of your partner's core values, fears, and dreams. The more you value and appreciate what matters to this person, the more your relationship will thrive.

The Fourth Pillar: Have a Shared Purpose

Working towards something that matters is not only intoxicating, it is a primarily source of life. Have you ever seen how some people just seem to be full of life? We can almost guarantee you that these people are that way because they know who they are and where they are going— even if they are very far away from their goal.

The bottom line is that purpose gives meaning; an overriding shared purpose and set of goals is the glue that holds a relationship together. This is *the* intangible factor that fuels continuance even in the face of significant doubt and frustration.

The Fifth Pillar: Quality Communication

The *quality* of your communication both shapes and determines the quality of your relationship. By quality, we are not referring to the amount of communication you have with your partner, or even the willingness to communicate. Quality communication only exists when the two people are mutually committed to both listening *and* being heard. Each must have the space to express differing points of view, feelings, or perceptions, and the desire to reach some mutual understanding or compromise even when agreement seems impossible.

To repeat, because it is vital and very misunderstood: **good communication does _not_ mean that you have to agree with everything your partner says or does. What it *does* mean is that both people**

are comfortable expressing how they feel or what they see, and both are committed to some mutual resolution when conflict is present. Sometimes that mutual resolution will mean one partner has to make compromises. Other times, both partners will need to make compromises in order to meet each other in the middle. Whatever the case, the two people never lose sight of the bigger picture and purpose and that they are making this journey together.

Eight Practices of Successful Couples: An Overview

Now that we have the fundamentals in place, it is time to get to the real core of what makes a relationship healthy, successful, and full of passion and intimacy on a day-to-day basis. One of the tools that we frequently use in our workshops is elevating awareness by asking "dynamic questions." These are questions that inspire one to explore the heart of any issue in a new context—revealing new insights and breakthroughs as a result. For example, here are two dynamic questions that helped us uncover some of the relationship principles found in this book:

1. *"What do couples think, say and do early on in a relationship that creates passion, excitement and real intimacy?"*

2. *"For couples who have been together awhile, and still display passion, excitement and real intimacy in their relationship, which of these early attitudes and practices are still present?*

Our primary insight was:

We have observed that the couples who manage to keep the excitement and passion alive in their primary relationship do so by simply continuing to act on and build on the strategies that worked from the beginning. They have learned how to integrate the practices that early on evoked passion, joy, and trust, and turn them into consistent relationship habits.

Let's pause so you can if possible, get your partner involved before you proceed. Let him or her catch up and digest the ideas that you have just read before you continue. As we mentioned above, while it only takes one person to be the catalyst, in order for a relationship to *flourish*, both need to be engaged in a shared vision.

Hopefully, you are both willing participants in this new journey. But, even if your significant other is having a hard time coming around, do not lose hope. Most relationships can be resuscitated through the efforts of one person operating as the catalyst for a new future. Your change in behavior and attitude often will bring your partner over to your side. Just be patient.

One last point before we begin outlining the key practices below. We suggest you go through these practices slowly and savor the moments and discoveries along the way. This is not a race, and there is no need to cram everything in. Take it one step at a time and one practice at a time. Any one practice can kick start an undeniable wellspring of goodwill and intimate connection.

As you consider each of these practices, ask yourselves:

"Is this practice something we did in the beginning that helped create the sizzle? Would it be fun to recommit to? Could this be a new idea that might be fun or valuable to practice with each other?"

Practice #1:
Focus on Appreciation

People in great relationships tend to focus on, accentuate, and celebrate the positive qualities that their partner possesses. Although they recognize their partner has faults, they do not let these things stand in the way of their relationship.

What we focus on is actually more of a choice than we realize. We can actively choose to focus on the positive or the negative in any person or any situation. Aspects of both will always be there; it is up to us to decide where we will put our attention.

We all want to be noticed and recognized for the good we bring to the world. Appreciation costs nothing, but it is an investment that rewards both the giver *and* the receiver. Both giving appreciation and feeling appreciated releases many of the same positive feelings we get when we are "in love." When we express gratefulness to and for our partner and the relationship we share, it both strengthens the relationship and evokes an experience of joy and love.

This practice is about specifically appreciating your partner. To set the stage, reflect on what it was that most attracted you to your partner at the beginning. Try to look past the faults for a few minutes. It is important that you rediscover and reconnect with the positive qualities that have always been present in your relationship and with your partner.

It is so easy to fall into the habit of taking your relationships and the people around you for granted! Even worse, we can get used to focusing on the negative. However, choosing to see the good side of your partner can be a habit, too! Once you really start to focus on how grateful you are to have this person in your life, you will notice a definite shift in the way you look at and feel about this person. And guess what? You may be amazed at how much your partner will "rise to the occasion" as a result. The more a person feels appreciated, the more that person will want to do the very things that generate the appreciation. This is a fundamental rule of human nature.

Some examples of the kinds of things you can appreciate and admire in your partner are:

- aspects of their personality
- what they are good at
- what they are working to improve
- what they do that makes a difference for other people
- their looks and physical appearance

(this applies to men just as much as women)

Action Plan for Practice #1

1. Ask yourself, *"What do I really appreciate and admire about my partner?"* Make a list of at least ten qualities you appreciate.

2. At least three times today, take about 30 seconds to think about the qualities you most appreciate most about your partner.

3. As you go about thinking how much you appreciate your partner, make sure you also let him/her know. If you are not physically in front of this person, then give them this message by way of a phone call, email, or text message. Let

your partner know in some way that you appreciate him/her for something every day.

4. At least once a week find a deeper or creative way to express your appreciation towards your partner. For example:

   a. Send a card expressing your feelings and appreciation for the contributions they make to your life

   b. Give a small gift that represents that you are thinking positively about him/her

   c. Make a gesture that shows you notice your partner's successes and struggles.

Practice #2:
Put Your Primary
Relationship First

Realize that the status of your closest, most intimate relationship will significantly affect your personal happiness as well as your ability to succeed in any of your life's endeavors. For this reason, you have a lot to benefit from making this relationship a top priority in your life. For us personally, aside from our relationship with Jesus Christ, there is nothing that is more important to us than the relationship we have with each other.

Napoleon Hill, in his landmark book, "Think and Grow Rich" wrote:

"No man is happy or complete without the modifying influence of the right woman (gender is neutral). He who does not recognize this important truth deprives himself of the power

which has helped men achieve greater success than all other forces combined."

Put simply, the energy that emanates between the couple is the reference point for everything else that happens. This does not mean that the couple cannot or should not do things separately from each other. It means that the relationship's physical, mental and emotional touchstones are the core from which everything else branches off.

Thus, the goal of this practice is to help you recognize and prioritize the importance of a successful and healthy primary relationship. In other words, your competing roles, jobs, hobbies, and other interests must take a back seat to your significant other in order to have a primary relationship that is sustainable and fulfilling.

Couples who are able to build a strong foundation and consistently make their relationship a priority are able to weather the challenges that threaten their sense of unity and connection to each other. These threats can come from outside the relationship, such as the demands of co-workers during a sudden business crisis or your children who often want their needs to be put first.

This same power struggle can occur with you or your partner's in-laws. Every wonder why there are so many "mother-in-law" jokes? If you think about them, they point toward the same underlying power struggle. When a struggle for power involves three or more parties, it is called "triangulation." Triangulation is a painful dysfunction that can lead to miscommunication and hurt feelings for couples and their families.

By putting your relationship first, you send a powerful message, not only to each other, but to those around you that you are a connected, committed, and loving couple who will not permit others to get in the middle.

When in the company of other adults (this includes noticing and interrupting people if they say something that paints your partner in a negative light) you can say something subtle like, "we all have things to work on, but for me he/she brings so much compassion to our relationship that I hardly notice." Or, it can be a firmer interruption such as, "we don't put each other down and I would appreciate it if you don't either." The key is to interrupt it the moment it happens and as neutrally as possible.

Action Plan for Practice #2

1. Sit down with each other and make this practice of "putting your relationship

first" an agreement that you are both willing to defend and stay aligned with— no matter what. It is powerful and affirming to acknowledge that nothing is more important to you and your happiness than your primary relationship!

2. Write a note, and put it where you will see it, exclaiming, *"I am committed to put my relationship with my spouse/partner ahead of my relationship with any other person and ahead of anything else in my life!"*

3. Become aware of the moments when *you* allow others to get their way or elevate their relationship with you by diminishing your relationship with your partner. As you become aware of it, interrupt and correct it immediately

without justifying it any further.

4. As a conscious practice, make it a habit to ask yourself how any major or even minor decisions may affect your partner *before* you make the decision. Even better, ask for your partner's input before you make decisions. This gives your partner the message that you value what he/she thinks and feels.

5. Frequently acknowledge and communicate to your partner that your relationship with him/her is the most important thing in your life.

Practice #3:
Associate your Partner with Pleasurable Experiences

As you go about building and strengthening your relationship, you want to associate an increasing number of pleasurable thoughts, feelings, and experiences with your partner. While this is something that will gain momentum over time, this third practice is about helping you get the process going.

Here are a couple of questions to help you assess how you currently feel about your partner. Answer them as honestly as possible:

1. "When I look at or think about my partner, what are the feelings that bubble up and the thoughts that immediately come to mind?"

The answer to this question can reveal a lot about the level of intimacy and passion that you and your partner are experiencing. Does your heart skip a beat, or leap for joy when you see or think about your partner? (If so, that is great!) Or, do you feel a twinge of dread? Perhaps, it is something in between?

2. Is the way you feel when you look at or think about your partner different from what it was when the two of you first got together?

If you answered "no," it could be for an assortment of reasons. You may be thinking:

I simply don't find myself very attracted to my partner any more. Sure, I love him/her, but he/she is older... fatter... meaner... which just isn't as appealing. But, it's not really bothering me that much. It's just the way it is.

I have grown to accept it.

No, you really do not have to just "accept it." The good news is there are some easy ways to both become more attractive to and attracted by your partner. Like anything else, attraction can be created and nurtured; you just have to commit yourself to make some necessary changes.

The following is a blueprint for generating pleasurable thoughts, feelings, and experiences between you and your partner.

1. Make being physically attractive for each other a conscious priority in your relationship.

There's the old joke in which a couple is standing at the altar and the minister says: "I now pronounce you man and wife. You may now let your bodies go to pot."

Remember when you first met? I am sure you put in a lot of effort to look nice for the other person. What about today? Are you still putting in that effort, and if the answer is "no," then why not?

It is so easy to become complacent in this area. Once couples have "attracted" their partner and entered into a long-term commitment, they can then take it for granted that their partner will always be attracted to them. They simply stop trying to impress and entice the other; the whole act somehow loses its significance and importance.

Yet, many of these same people will continue to put in an effort to look nice for *other people—* even people they hardly know. It really does not make sense, does it?

If you are guilty of being lax in this area then *now* is the time to renew your commitment to being physically attractive to your partner and make it a priority in your life. You can start with these simple steps:

1. When you are around your partner, dress to the same standard you would with anyone you want to impress
2. Pay special attention to your grooming
3. Commit yourself to a healthy diet and drink plenty of water
4. Maintain a body weight and tone that makes you look and feel attractive
5. Exercise at least 3 times a week

Discuss your plan with your partner, and if your partner is up for it, you can create a plan together and help each other maintain it. If you feel that you cannot talk to your partner about this then just start with yourself. It will not be long before the other person will take notice and it may be the catalyst that encourages this person to improve him/herself as well.

The key is to commit to looking and feeling your best as often as possible. You are not only going to feel better, but you will elevate your energy to a higher level which will cause you to be more attractive to the rest of the world as well!

2. Change your mental associations.

I want you to close your eyes and think about your partner. Notice the images and feelings that are evoked. Are they are primarily positive or negative?

When we are in a particular mental state— happy, excited, sad, etc.—and an event is simultaneously experienced, our brain tends to make a link between the two. It is a process called "mental anchoring." This experience is bundled as a picture with the attached emotions and stored or "anchored" in your subconscious mind.

Unless you have an unusual capacity to live in the present moment, you are not really experiencing events and people as they are; you are experiencing them according to your subconscious mental models.

Here are a couple of examples:

Let's say you are driving on the freeway and you hear a siren behind you. You probably begin to tense up and your heart begins to race. Why? At some point you have made the mental association between driving a car, the sound of a siren, with possibly getting a speeding ticket.

So, if you find yourself in that same circumstance, you would immediately feel anxious, and your heart will begin to race. All of these reactions occur within your subconscious mind—on autopilot.

Businesses take advantage of mental anchoring and exploit it mercilessly. Have you ever noticed how many TV commercials seem to have very little to do with the product the advertisers are actually selling? Consider your typical car and beer commercials.

The intent of the commercial is to get you in a particular emotional state. For example, they may create a funny scene that makes you laugh and feel good. Then, while you are in that "feeling good" place, the name of the product appears on the screen. Their goal is to make your mind associate the experience of feeling good with their product.

They know that if you watch the commercial a few times, there will be a deepened and reinforced association between those positive feelings and their product—so much so that the next time you are in the store it will affect your buying decision. As you scan the shelves looking at all the choices, you will recognize the product from the commercial, and bingo, you will start to feel good! You may not even know why you instinctively favor that brand of beer over the others; you simply choose to buy it.

So how relevant is all of this to your relationships? Consider the following:

> *Tom is driving home after work. He has had a busy and stressful day at the office. The traffic on the way home is heavy. As he crawls along in the traffic, he listens to several*

rather gloomy news reports on the radio. When he finally arrives home and walks in his front door, he is in a bad mood. While in this negative state, the first person he sees is his wife...

Worse, this same scenario is repeated 2-3 times a week.

Can you see what can end up happening over here? By repeatedly being exposed to his wife while in a negative state, Tom's wife can literally *become* a negative anchor! This means that over time Tom can get into a bad mood by merely looking at his wife.

When you are in a relationship, you will experience your partner while you are in various mental and emotional states. This is especially true when you live together. You no longer always get to choose to be with him/her only when you are feeling happy and excited, sexy or energetic. This means you need to become aware of the moments or behaviors that may be creating negative anchors and learn how to avoid them or at least minimize their impact. Simultaneously, you want to learn how to recognize and build upon the positive anchors. When, for example, was the last time you actually smiled at your partner, and how often have you smiled at him/her over the past week? How often do you two laugh together?

You may be surprised by how much of a difference both consistently smiling at and laughing with your partner can make!

In order to change and limit the negative associations between you and your partner, here are some well tested tips:

1. If you find yourself in a bad mood try to get some distance from your partner. If that is not possible, then simply let him/her know you are in a bad mood and you need a little space. This statement also sends an alert to your mind that *you* should not be linking your mood to your partner.

2. When you are not around your partner, get into the habit of thinking positive thoughts about him/her. You can use the strategies in Practice #1 on appreciation to elicit positive anchors.

3. When you are feeling happy, excited and energized, make an effort to physically be next to your partner. If that is not possible, then bring your partner to your conscious mind and ask your mind to associate your partner with that feeling.

4. When you are doing an activity with your partner and you notice that you are enjoying yourself, savor the experience and consciously pause and ask your mind to associate this moment and feelings with your relationship.

5. Physical touch can elicit a full range of feelings and emotions. You of course want your physical touch to be associated with pleasure. Make it a daily habit to lovingly touch or caress your partner's face, head, or neck, or hold his/her hand. The important point is to find what works. You want to locate those areas where your partner wants and enjoys being touched physically.

By understanding the way your brain works, you can train yourself to literally create the emotions you really want. It is one of the most powerful ways to build and maintain a great relationship!

Action Plan for Practice #3

1. Repeat the five steps mentioned above about making being physically attractive to your partner a priority.

2. Repeat the five steps mentioned above about creating positive mental associations with your partner while avoiding the negative anchors.

3. Smile at your partner at least three times each and every day. Make it a big, broad grin that shows you are happy that he/she is there.

4. When you are having a good time with

your partner, work to be in the moment. Experience it as fully as you can and savor it.

5. Commit to at least one fun activity a week with your partner.

6. Make it a daily habit to lovingly touch or caress your partner's face, head, or neck, or hold his/her hand. The important point is to find what works for you and your partner in order to create a pleasurable experience.

Practice #4:
Be Fully Present In Your Relationship

Though this practice may seem pretty straight forward, the truth is most of us going through life on autopilot. It is not just that we are buried in our thoughts—worrying about what just happened or what might happen in the future—we also minimize disruptions by shutting out a growing pack of outside distractions competing for our attention.

For instance, have you ever seen a couple sitting in a restaurant or out on a walk together, and the two of them are so busy with their Smartphone that they hardly speak to each other, let alone even so much as give a glance in the other's direction?

When it comes to relationships, not being in

the *here and now* with our mind and body has a negative impact. It sends a loud and clear message that the person you are (barely) pretending to be with, or listening to, is not very important.

In contrast, have you ever had the experience of being with someone who was interested in, and in tune with, what you were saying? Not only did you feel good as a result, but this person became more attractive to you as well. Those who are present and available in their interactions with other people are rare and valuable, which is why it is always valuable to be one of these people.

Being present in your experiences with your partner will have a big impact on your relationship. When you are with this person and he/she is talking, make an effort to fully pay attention to what is being said. This means keeping your thoughts focused on the conversation as well. As you look at your partner, really try to connect to who this person is. If there is physical contact, concentrate on feeling his/her touch and yours.

To put these ideas into practice, develop the habit of stopping any external activity that is competing for your attention while you are communicating with someone. Put down your magazine, turn off your cell phone, turn off the TV, and bring your awareness to the human being that is in front of you.

Action Plan for Practice #4

1. Practice being present when you are alone. Notice the thoughts going on in your head and how they take your attention away from being able to really experience what is going on with you

and around you right now.

2. Find a meditation technique that appeals to you, and practice it for a couple of minutes each day. Meditation is a great mechanism to build personal presence.

3. When your partner is saying something to you, stop whatever else you are doing and bring all of your attention to this person.

4. Stay present and connected when you are with your partner. Notice all the details about how this person looks. When he/she speaks, really listen to what your partner is sharing with you.

Practice #5:
Embrace What Is

Having worked with numerous couples, one pattern that we keep seeing over and over again is that **what worked in the beginning of the relationship will likely continue to work indefinitely**. The problem is that most people abandon what worked in the beginning—not because these strategies or thought patterns stopped working, but because somewhere along the way one or both of the people shifted their focus from embracing "what is" and practicing acceptance, to judging and resisting.

In our workshops, people will occasionally ask for a definition of "love." Is it a feeling? A way of being? A commitment?

Our answer is that **love is inextricably**

connected to our knowledge and acceptance of those around us. It is an outcome of our conscious effort to appreciate what the other is good at while accepting this person's current limitations and struggles. It is about actively embracing the entire package of who someone is—the good *and* the bad.

Think back to when you fell in love or when you felt most in love. I am willing to bet you were highly accepting of your partner's interests and behaviors. Things that irritate you today about your partner did not always bother you. In the beginning you just accepted everything as part of the package. You embraced the quirks and the lapses in judgment. You were patient, tolerant, and forgiving.

Are you as generous today?

Your generosity worked in your favor. Your

willingness to accept who your partner is, and more importantly, who your partner is not, is the key to keeping the feelings we call "falling in love or "being in love," alive and constant.

Science tells us we project the parts of ourselves that we do not like onto others. This means if you do not like judgmental people, it is because you do not like the part of yourself that is judgmental. Or if you do not enjoy being around those who are seemingly insincere, it is because you do not like the part of yourself that is inauthentic. All you need to do to be more accepting of your partner is to be more accepting of *yourself*! So, begin the work of embracing and forgiving yourself for the parts of your own personality and behavior that you dislike. Soon those exact traits will no longer bother you, and you will stop judging *others* negatively for having them as well.

Action Plan for Practice #5

1. Create a list of everything that irritates you about your partner. (Keep in mind that this is a *list*, not a book.) For each item on the list, ask yourself what is the quality that you are attaching to this behavior? For example, if you feel your partner is spending too much money on a hobby, the quality you might be attaching to that behavior is "selfishness" or "being wasteful." You will end up with a list of qualities that are bothering you.

   Now, go through this list, and for each quality, bring to mind times in your recent past where you have exhibited that same quality yourself. Once you own it, commit to forgiving yourself for having that quality, and forgive yourself for any harm it may have caused. Once a week continue to repeat this process until these qualities *feel* neutral— especially when you experience them in your partner.

2. Each day for a couple of weeks make a list of any negative judgments you had in regard to your partner. For each of these negative judgments, find something else related, yet positive to focus on instead.

3. Practice noticing who your partner is for others. Look for ways to consciously appreciate what you are noticing.

4. In those moments when you notice that your partner is not doing what you *think* he/she should be doing; focus instead on what your partner is currently doing

that is making a difference for you or others.

5. Repeat the following mantra to yourself as many times as you need until it feels natural: "I choose to love and accept [your partner's name] and everything that goes with him/her—the good and the bad. He/she also choose to love and accept me and everything about me—the good and the bad."

Practice #6:
Discover What Matters

One of the most exciting aspects of any intimate relationship, especially at the beginning, is discovering what matters to your partner. You will find that the more values that you have in common, the greater your feelings of connection and excitement tend to be.

The way that we experience the world is noticeably influenced by our system of values. Values are those qualities, beliefs and attitudes that we prioritize as being the most important to us. The exact combination of values that a person possesses is different for every individual.

Not surprisingly, values play an important role in our most intimate relationships. The people who are able to tune in to those around them out what truly matters to the other

e often the ones who are the most successful in their intimate relationships.

If you are lacking in this area, then it is a quality that you should develop. Think of it as an ongoing treasure hunt. You will begin to discover and connect to not only what those around you are saying, but more importantly, why they are saying it. When you are in this kind of listening mode, you will start to realize what motivates the people you are most connected to, what pushes their buttons, what they love to talk about, and what you can contribute to their lives that will be especially valuable to them.

In all great primary relationships, two things need to be in place when it comes to discovering what matters:

1. You must have at least some values in common with your partner.

2. Where your values are in conflict, you must find ways to meet your partner's needs through **their** set of values.

If you are unsure what values you and your partner possess, here is a list of some commonly held personal values:

Adventure

Creativity

Honesty

Loyalty

Generosity

Self-Control

Sacrifice

Faith

Peace

Love

Security

Learning

Simplicity

Health

Beauty

Freedom

Spirituality

Friendship

Contribution

Sense of

belonging

Devotion to

Family

Fun

While the above list above is far from exhaustive, you should take some time to read through it, add other obvious values, and use it as a springboard to make a list of your own personal core values. Once you have created this list, narrow it down to your top five values by asking yourself, "If I eliminate this value as a priority, how much would it affect the quality of my life and my relationships?" Ask your partner to do the same, and make some quality time together to go through both lists.

As you go through the lists together, you may begin to see clues that clearly point to when and why conflicts occur between you and your partner. **Conflicts are always the result of a conflict in values.**

As an illustration of how a conflict can arise, think of a time when you did something for your partner, such as preparing a nice meal, buying a gift, or going out somewhere, and the other person did not seem to really appreciate the gesture in the way you hoped he/she would. Your partner likely reacted that way either because the experience or the gift you gave did not quite match up with what matters to him/her, or it conflicted with something else that matters almost as much or more.

For example, say you were to take your partner to an expensive restaurant for dinner. It is in a lovely setting, you have not been there before. The food is very inventive—all things that you value. While you are there, you order an expensive bottle of wine to share.

If your partner's system of values around money, food, and enjoying expensive gifts are different to yours, then this could end up creating a conflict. And, if you are paying attention, you will hear the source of the conflict in the statements that your partner makes:

"This is very expensive – can we really afford it?"

"The wine better be great for all that

money."

"We could have used the money for something more practical that we really need."

If you knew what mattered most to your partner, you might have created the experience you wanted by ordering a burger with fries and eating them on the beach!

When we are listening for and paying attention to what matters to our partner we can:

1. Find ways to create experiences for the other person that he/she will truly enjoy.
2. Express what **we** want as it relates to what matters to the other person.

Using the above examples, that give you two workable approaches, you could have either:

1. Arranged an impromptu dinner of burger and fries on the beach because that is what your partner would appreciate and relate to, or...

2. Immediately framed the purpose of the evening. You could have shared why you chose the restaurant and why you felt that it was important to splurge in this instance. For example, you wanted your partner to experience being appreciated in an extravagant way.

While it may seem obvious why the first approach would work, what about the second approach? The reason why the second approach can be effective is due to the fact that you started off by acknowledging and validating your partner's values, then clearly explained why you decided to deviate from those values in this situation.

Another important point to keep in mind is that when we say we do not like doing something, often it is not the actual activity that we do not like. Sometimes what we really dislike is the meaning we associate with the activity. For example, your partner may say that he/she does not like white water rafting. It could be that your partner values safety, security, or peace of mind and considers white water rafting to be a risky activity. Thus, white water rafting is not going to give your partner what he/she wants!

But, what if you happen to enjoy white water rafting and would like to do it together with your partner? It is still possible? Yes! But, it will only work if you can help your partner find a way to have his/her values met in that activity. Then, your partner may have different feelings about it. So, you could focus instead on all the safety precautions that will be taken. You could also give your partner a comfortable level of control over certain aspects of the trip, such as which routes you will travel. Finally, you could focus on other facets of the experience that your partner will relate to, such as the peace and serenity of being out in nature.

Action Plan for Practice #6

1. Discover your five highest values.

2. Discover your partner's five highest values.

3. Take some time to go over the two lists together with your partner. Determine which values you share in common. Are there any that seemingly conflict?

4. Plan an activity for your partner with elements that meet his or her highest values.

5. Practice listening for what matters in your conversations with your partner. Repeat back the part that matters so

your partner can validate that you understand.

6. When you are planning something with your partner, focus the conversation on what you think matters about the activity that reflects your partner's core values.

Practice #7:
Choosing to Let Go

It happens to the best of relationships. There is a misspoken word, a misunderstanding occurs, or a lie is told. Unconsciously the walls go up, silent resentment builds, and suddenly the years of friendship, love and positive memories disappear. Rather quickly, either or both now find themselves adrift in a sea of hurt, confusion and disbelief. We have all been there at one time or another.

For many, this marks the beginning of the end of their relationship. The good news is that these experiences are transformable and can instead be the beginning of a breakthrough in terms of intimacy and connection. The practice of forgiving, coupled with authentically being able to let go of past hurts, is a necessary element for a healthy relationship.

We all know the basic definition of forgiveness, but I want to add to it. Forgiveness enables us to authentically "give as before." It happens when you joyfully give your love, time, laughter, kindness, patience, compassion, etc. as you did before the painful event pain took place. I believe that such forgiveness is a gift that every person needs access to because it can literally change the quality of not only your life, but of those around you.

The ability to forgive allows us the opportunity to experience being a giver once more. It not only frees the heart and soul, it gives birth to a new reality where both people can now give and receive as they once did with each other.

*To forgive is to set a prisoner free
and discover that the prisoner was you.*
-Lewis B. Smedes

To help you and your partner reach a true level of forgiveness, here is a question for you to consider:

Have you forgiven *yourself?*

Quite often the anger and bitterness that prevents us from forgiveness is the belief that we are the ones who caused the experience to happen.

Whether or not this is actually true, the sense of guilt or shame that we feel may be the very reason we cannot get to the point of forgiving the other person. In other words, **until we learn to forgive ourselves, we will not be able to forgive others.**

In our many years of experience and working with both individuals and couples, self-forgiveness seems to be a rare practice. Yet, those who *do* practice it have experiences that are profound and extremely liberating.

Ok, so how do you even begin forgiving yourself?

The first step would be to locate the part *you* played in the negative situations or experiences in your adult life.

For example, we have worked with many adults who had a suspicion that their spouse was having an affair, yet instead of having the difficult conversation; they chose to ignore it and hoped it would simply go away. We have worked with women who felt that their partner was a little too physical with the children and decided to ignore their feelings because there were so many other positive qualities within this person—only to find out years later of the debilitating and constant abuse the children had suffered under their watchful eye. We know of businessmen and women who paid little attention to their financial affairs and later paid the price when both their bank accounts and trust were literally and figuratively depleted.

In each of these situations, the offended person somehow witnessed or sensed something was amiss and chose to ignore what was evident. Their realization that they should have done something different is why they have such a difficult time forgiving themselves. They are haunted by thoughts of, "I knew it...I just didn't want to believe it," or "I just didn't want him/her to think I didn't trust him/her"...

In most cases, if you are being honest with yourself, you will be able to remember the moment you chose to look the other way, and in a very real sense, promoted the undesired, yet inevitable outcome.

So first things first.... Make the acknowledgement and then stop blaming yourself! The situation *is* what it *is*. You now have the choice to either stay where you are, or move forward... Again, if you have chosen to read this book, then that means somewhere inside of yourself, you want to take the path that moves you forward in a positive, healthy way. We encourage you to give in to that urge.

Keep in mind that there is no right or wrong way to forgive yourself or others. What is critical is that it be authentic and that you allow yourself to truly let go of the hurt, pain and blame so that you can move on with your life.

How to do it? There are many ways of forgiving yourself. Saying affirmative statements out loud is helpful. Sharing with someone you trust *with the intent to let go* works as well. Some, by turning to prayer find the relief they are seeking. We often recommend writing everything down on a piece of paper and then burning the paper.]

Whatever you end up doing, please know that it takes courage to say what needs to be said and to no longer allow self doubt and blame to hold you hostage, and dictate your life.

Once you have begun the process of self forgiveness, you can then begin forgiving those closest to you—particularly your spouse or partner. To get that process going, consider the following questions. Please answer each one as honestly as you can.

1. Do you truly want to forgive your partner? Why?

2. Are there any benefits to holding on to the anger, resentment, etc., such as seeking attention or sympathy from others?

3. Is forgiving this act/situation/event nonnegotiable to the survival of this relationship? Why?

4. If you were to forgive, what would you gain or recover by forgiving and letting go?

5. Could your forgiveness change the other's life? How?

6. What are the ramifications for both of you if you do not forgive?

7. Who else does your unwillingness to forgive impact? In what way?

8. Do you like who you become when you do not forgive? Describe.

9. Would you like to experience yourself as an empowered forgiver and move on joyfully with your life? Describe.

10. What could be different in this relationship because of your choice to forgive?

As you answer these questions, notice if you have any competing thoughts, for example, "I want to forgive, but what if he/she does it again?" Or, "I want to forgive, but I don't want him/her to think I am a pushover." If you have any of these thoughts, then here is something else you need to consider:

Neither you nor I control what others do, say,

feel, or think. Yet we can influence their choices. The most powerful way to influence people's choices around you is to get clear about who you are, what you truly value, and what you will accept and not accept within your relationship, and then live in a way that others "get it."

In other words, if you want to forgive, then forgive. Do not worry about how he/she is interpreting your forgiveness or what this person will do with it. Your partner will do what he/she does. Forgiveness is about you letting go and then responsibly living and experiencing yourself and your life in a way that brings you authentic joy.

However you choose to forgive, the first thing you will want to acknowledge is that you **can** forgive and that the first person this process will benefit is you. Forgiveness is simply a choice, and it has always been *your* choice. It is precisely at this point that true freedom begins!

Action Plan for Practice #7

1. Recognize the part that you have played in the situations or experiences in your adult life that you are having a hard time letting go of.

2. Commit yourself to achieving self-forgiveness, and determine the strategies for letting go that work best for you.

3. Answer the 10 questions about forgiving others as honestly as you can.

4. Make the decision to forgive those closest to you regardless of what you imagine their reaction will be.

Practice #8: Keep the Goodwill Basket Full

All couples, including those with the most loving and connected relationships, have disagreements and occasionally fight. Realize that it is an inseparable part of a healthy relationship. So, if you want a great relationship, the goal is not to avoid disagreements, but to learn how to have those disagreements without damaging the connection you share with your partner.

**Healthy couples disagree and fight
in ways that preserve
both the relationship and their
respect for each other.**

While healthy disagreement may look different for different couples, what all great couples have in common is that they are very aware that retaliatory statements and actions can have long-term damaging effects. They possess sufficient self-control, awareness, and emotional maturity to bite their tongue when they are about to cross a line that will likely damage their partner or the relationship. They just do not blurt out what feels good when they are in the middle of an argument. They have a voice in their head that says, "Don't say it! You are just angry right now, and you will live to regret it!" They exhibit enough emotional intelligence to communicate in a way that any potential damage is minimized.

Even a good relationship can quickly deteriorate when both partners are caught up in the quest to be right. While being right can feel validating, the need to be right fundamentally destroys relationships. It is important to learn to harness your ego, which when feeling threatened, wants to defend, or "win" at all costs. The consequence of lashing out is, your partner will likely shut down, learn to withhold his/her opinions, and will not associate you with pleasure.

If you find that you are struggling in this area, here is a practice that will help. Just before you start or escalate a disagreement into an argument, go into a room by yourself or turn to the side and say or think the following:

"I can either be 'right' or have this relationship work."

Making the choice to let go of being right in any given moment, and instead focusing on the big picture of your relationship, is something that always pays dividends down the road.

One hidden secret is that unconsciously, choices involving the other usually hinge on the amount of goodwill that exists in the relationship.

In a successful relationship <u>both</u> partners are focused on giving much more than they are taking.

Keep in mind, I do not mean "giving in" to the other; I mean "giving *to*" the other. Building and maintaining goodwill is critical for the long term success of any relationship.

Think of an imaginary basket that is placed between you and your partner. Each of you is able to make positive emotional deposits in this basket. If you will implement the practices mentioned above, the basket will fill quickly and stay full. And, that is exactly what you want to happen. Here's why...

As an adult, you likely realize that life may not necessarily play out in the way that you want it to. While there may be some areas in our lives that we can control, there are many, many, other areas that are simply out of our hands. One such area is our partner's reaction to distressful or unpleasant events. All that goodwill you built up, one deposit at a t can be pulled out by the handful when turbulence hits. In other words, this basket is like a bank account; it builds up gradually, but depletes quickly when times are tough.

Keeping the goodwill basket full is about focusing on giving to your partner and causing positive experiences on a consistent daily basis so that it will remain well filled during the difficult times.

This is one of the most sustainable practices we have given you. Too often a relatively strong relationship ends just because no one was making consistent deposits into the basket. One minute everything seems fine until, swoosh, in goes the hand into an empty basket, and suddenly the relationship is on the rocks because it appears not to be worth it any more. Never let a relationship die because you took more than you gave.

Action Plan for Practice #8

1. Set aside a few minutes today to just to be with your partner—go for a walk or a drive.

2. Come up with at least three new things you could do together to develop a shared positive experience—do at least one.

3. Think of ways to enrich the experiences you already share together.

4. Make a conscious effort to add more than you take from your relationship basket each day.

5. Find a way to demonstrate kindness toward your partner each day. It might be the tone of your voice or a small gesture that would make your partner happy.

Implementing the 8 Practices

Now that we have covered the 8 fundamental practices of a successful relationship, here are some tips on how you and your partner can best implement them:

1. Take action.

Although you may find this book interesting, if you really want to renew your relationship, then you have to act on the ideas and strategies contained herein. Even if you are not convinced that one or more of these practices will work for you—give it a try anyway. None of the practices are difficult, and each will help to restore your relationship to the vibrancy it once had.

2. Give the process the time it needs.

Changing a behavior or habit takes both time and diligence. You can easily sabotage your efforts by attempting to do everything at once. So make sure you work on just one practice per week. Start with Practice #1 and go through the Action Plan provided for that practice. The following week, work on Practice #2. In eight weeks after you have experimented with each practice, start again at Practice #1. By doing a little each day you will be AMAZED how much things will change in a surprisingly short period of time.

New habits are not often formed quickly; the more difficult the practice, the longer it will take for the practice to become second nature. In this book, we have made a conscious effort to keep the practices simple by reducing them to their most basic elements. Nevertheless, you may find that some of them take longer to fully implement than others.

3. Create a system to remind yourself of

your goal.

Even if you only focus on one practice per week, it is very easy to get caught up in life and forget about these commitments completely. One way to remind yourself about each practice is to keep your practice of the week on a card and carry it with you at all times. Whatever you do, find a way to keep it at the top of your mind until the behaviors become natural and habitual.

4. Discuss the habits with your partner if possible.

Practicing these strategies with your partner or spouse can make the effects much more powerful. In fact, sharing this book with your partner, discussing each practice together, and encouraging each other can totally transform your relationship. If you feel, however, that your partner will not be open to the idea, or he/she expresses no interest, do not give up.

These practices can still work even without your partner's participation. In this case, it usually will not take long before your partner notices a change in the dynamic of your relationship and responds to you in a positive way.

5. Keep a journal of your progress.

Another great idea is to keep a record of your progress as you begin to implement these new practices. Get into the habit of writing down or typing any noticeable changes in you or your partner no matter how small or insignificant they may seem. This can include you and your partner's feelings and attitudes, your thoughts, and anything new that happens as a result of applying each practice. You may feel that the changes are gradual. But when you look back through all the entries you have made, you will get a real sense of just how far you have come.

6. Be persistent.

Give each of these practices some time to take effect. Push yourself to stay consistent and conscious of which practice you are putting into action. Do not just try a practice once or twice. Instead, work to turn each one into a lasting habit.

7. Use the suggested Action Plan provided for each habit.

At the end of each chapter, you will see an Action Plan—a suggested series of steps to start making these practices a habit. These are the same steps that we have used to successfully help many couples just like you. So, use them—they work!

8. Celebrate your successes

When you notice that a change in your behavior has become easy, celebrate any renewed intimacy and passion in your relationship. After all, this is your goal. Reward yourself for what you achieve!

Conclusion

Realize that very few people take the time to focus on their relationship with the goal of improving it. Of those who will purchase this book, not everyone will actually read it, and the number who will both read it and apply it may unfortunately be an extremely small percentage. So, be proud of yourself for choosing to be in this elite group!

Just a few last closing thoughts:

1. None of the practices in this book are difficult or complicated. A couple of them might require a bit of creative thinking, but there is nothing here that requires any particular knowledge or skill.

2. These practices really are the things that most, **new** relationships tend to naturally have in place. But, most couples simply stop doing them, and the quality of their intimacy diminishes.

3. By being consciously aware of each practice, you have the power to make them a part of your life and to massively increase the quality of your relationship.

4. Focus and do each practice until they become habits. If you persistently apply them, it will not be long before they become second nature.

Afterword

If you enjoyed this book, then we know you would love our Breaking Through Workshops. You can attend these workshops as a couple or on your own. This program will give you advanced and sustainable practices for success in all of your relationships. You will learn to clarify your purpose, let go of limitations, and consciously manifest the results and experiences you are seeking in life. Also, if you would like private relationship coaching reach out to Nora at Nora@ZarvosCoaching.com

For more information and to register, please visit our website at www.ZarvosCoaching.com.

About The Authors

Nora Zarvos L.C.S.W. received her Bachelor's degree in Education and her Masters degree in Social Work. Nora's accomplishments include founding a transformational coaching and training company in Spain, as well as Zarvos Leadership & Coaching in Indianapolis. She is a recognized relationship expert and expert facilitator and loves inspiring women to new levels of fulfillment and leadership.

Contact Nora at Nora@ZarvosCoaching.com

Jim Zarvos has trained and coached over 50,000 students in the art of dynamic living and emotional intelligence. He is a global thought leader on relationships and leadership. Along with his wife Nora, he is the co-founder of Zarvos Leadership & Coaching. He is passionate about helping couples realize trusting, intimate relationships and experience true success and fulfillment.

Contact Jim at Jim@ZarvosCoaching.com

74182397R00068

Made in the USA
Middletown, DE
21 May 2018